Daily Dose with Dupé

100 quotes to help you jump-start your day
with positivity and inspiration

Dupé Aleru

Daily Dose with Dupé

100 quotes to help you jump-start your day with positivity and inspiration

Copyright © 2021 Dupé Aleru

ISBN: 978-0-9993214-3-0

Cover Illustration by Faith Clancy

For more information, visit www.dupealeru.com.

Daily Dose with Dupé

To you, courageous and strong human, thank you for being unapologetically you.

Introduction

I am happy that you're here because that means you have made a conscious decision to no longer allow your limiting beliefs, attitudes, and behaviors keep you from reaching your full potential. You have taken a courageous step on your journey towards personal development. Celebrate this moment as a commitment to discovering your true self. What do you want to achieve in life? What are you willing to sacrifice to achieve it? What routines and daily actionable steps will you need to establish so that you can reach your goals?

The first step in creating new opportunities is to shift your mindset into a growth mindset. What are you feeding your mind every day? What are your morning rituals? This is the time to be completely honest and transparent with yourself because if you are not able to recognize the poor habits that have been holding you back, then you will not be able to create good habits that will ignite a burning desire driving you forward.

Do you wake up in the morning and immediately grab your phone, endlessly scrolling through filtered posts, or do you roll over, hit the snooze button, squeezing out every ounce of sleep that you can muster? Are you the early bird, waking up to mediate, pray, workout, and feed your mind with positivity before you start your day?

I ask because I truly believe that the way you start your day greatly impacts your mindset, attitude, energy, and ability (or inability) to conquer daily challenges. If you are serious about creating the life that you desire and know you deserve, then complete this short assignment before moving on to the quotes section of the book.

Assignment:

What are 2 to 5 things that you can do every morning that will "fill you up" so you can tackle your daily goals? Understand this: it is impossible to pour from an empty cup. If your cup is empty and you do not fill it up before you head off to work, get the kids ready for school, or run errands, you will be performing at a lower intensity. Are you not convinced? Picture your smartphone. When the battery is at 20%, it still works, but a 20% charge for most people will not get you through the day. At some point, you will need to recharge the phone to full charge so it's ready for use during your entire day. The same goes for you. When you wake up, make sure you are fully charged before you step out into the world. Do this by consistently performing your morning rituals. Set your morning routine today, whether it's prayer, meditation, reading for 30 minutes, taking a walk, listening to motivational content, or reading a devotional.

I hope that this book will serve as part of your morning ritual—a motivational guide to help jump-start your day, adding a dose of positivity and awareness so that you can create the life you desire.

"The law of attraction is a beautiful phenomenon. If you attract what you think about the most, then you can decide to focus on possibilities to create more opportunities."

- Dupé Aleru

"A setback is when you fall but bounce back. Failure is when you quit with no intention of trying again."

- Dupé Aleru

"You will either win or lose. Either way, the direction of your life will depend on what you choose."

— Dupé Aleru

"It's not about being cocky. It's about having the confidence and self-awareness to do something greater than yourself that will leave an imprint in other people's hearts."

- Dupé Aleru

"Selfishness only sees itself."

- Dupé Aleru

"Sometimes letting go shows greater strength than holding onto what's destroying you."

- Dupé Aleru

"Those who did not see your vision will be the ones blinded by your mission."

- Dupé Aleru

"One of the fastest ways to discourage yourself is to compare your manuscript to someone else's publication."

- Dupé Aleru

"Do not allow your past pain to block your future purpose."

- Dupé Aleru

"A missed opportunity can be a missed legacy."

- Dupé Aleru

"Life may not give you unlimited chances to make your dreams come true. When opportunity comes knocking, you better be waiting by the door and open that [bleep] like it's Christmas morning."

- Dupé Aleru

"When you do not forgive others, you are
not hurting them, you are hurting yourself by
blocking your blessings. Forgiveness releases
people of their offense while
freeing up your future."

- Dupé Aleru

====================================

"The world doesn't owe you anything, but you owe it to yourself; to be the best you can be."

- Dupé Aleru

"Success does not happen overnight, no matter how someone's life is perceived to be. You must work your face off and see yourself achieving that goal to win."

- Dupé Aleru

"The only cure for jealousy is self-confidence and reframing one's thoughts."

- Dupé Aleru

"Excuse your excuses and
welcome your actions."

- Dupé Aleru

"You will not attract what you want unless you're willing to let go of what no longer serves you."

– Dupé Aleru

"If you have to question it, it ain't it."

- *Dupé Aleru*

"You did not fail; you fell. Dust yourself off, stand up, and try again."

- Dupé Aleru

"Deciding how you want to be remembered will help you determine what kind of life you will live today."

- Dupé Aleru

"The great thing about not liking where
you are in life is having another
chance to change it."

- Dupé Aleru

"Stand strong in your purpose and never allow anyone to tell you it's impossible."

- *Dupé Aleru*

"You do not have to tell everyone your dreams.
Show them. Place your energy
into working hard, and your success
will speak for itself."

_____
_____

- Dupé Aleru

"Never risk a long-term, healthy relationship
for short-term gratification."

– Dupé Aleru

"Your present life is a direct reflection of the choices you have made. If you want to reap different results, you need to sow different seeds."

- Dupé Aleru

"Their success wasn't set before you to make you envious; it was to give you the fuel to keep going."

– Dupé Aleru

"You own the rights to your life story. Do not allow people to infringe upon what has already been written for your advancement."

────────────────────────────

- Dupé Aleru

"There will be people who want to see you fail, while others will want to see you prevail."

– Dupé Aleru

"It is impossible to change the world without changing yourself first. Self-accountability and personal development are essential principles of change."

- Dupé Aleru

"You will miss the small blessings that come your way if you are always looking down."

- Dupé Aleru

"Sometimes people will be in disagreement with you not because what you're saying isn't true, but because your truth triggers their denial and unwillingness to change."

- Dupé Aleru

"Stop sleeping through your dreams. Wake up from them and begin living."

- Dupé Aleru

"Kiss your past goodbye and let your future catch it."

- Dupé Aleru

"Let your main focus be to remain focused."

- Dupé Aleru

"Never underestimate a person who is starving for success because there will be no leftovers."

———————————————————————

- Dupé Aleru

"Grind every day like it's your last, and you will accomplish your goals faster than you think."

- Dupé Aleru

"Sometimes people don't know how to help themselves, so it is easier for them to pass their pain onto others than it is to admit they need help."

- *Dupé Aleru*

"They call it being bossy, you call it being a boss. They say you are aggressive, you say it's confidence. If you allow other people to place their limiting beliefs and insecurities on you, you will find yourself lowering your standards to fit into places you do not belong."

- Dupé Aleru

"Procrastination is like eating a box of donuts. It feels good until you look at yourself in the mirror."

- Dupé Aleru

"There is no rewind button in life. You can either play it forward or throw away the tape."

- Dupé Aleru

"Overdeliver, and you will command attention."

- Dupé Aleru

"I want to inspire people. I want someone 20 years from now to look back and say, 'Because of you, I found my purpose and, in doing so, I was able to impact others.'"

- *Dupé Aleru*

"Jealousy is rooted in feelings
of inadequacy."

- Dupé Aleru

"You're not paranoid or confused. Your gut is pointing you in the right direction."

- Dupé Aleru

"You will never appreciate being on top of the world unless you know what it feels like to be at the bottom."

- Dupé Aleru

"If they do not like you yet, still keep up with everything you do; they are a supporter."

- Dupé Aleru

"Never stop doing what you love just because someone else hasn't figured out who they are."

- Dupé Aleru

"Sometimes, all you need to do is show up for your life to level up."

- Dupé Aleru

"You will never be able to please everyone, so don't stress yourself trying."

- Dupé Aleru

"When you know your worth, you will stop putting your talents on layaway when your ideal customers are fully capable of paying in full."

- *Dupé Aleru*

"Be courageous enough to walk away from people and situations that no longer serve your purpose."

_____

- Dupé Aleru

"Your perception of yourself can either propel you forward or hold you back. Your life will resemble your thoughts, so be mindful of the words you speak into the Universe."

- Dupé Aleru

"The question shouldn't be "Why me?" The question should be, "Why not me?" I was given the toughest challenge because I can conquer it."

- Dupé Aleru

"Be the type of energy that you want to see in the world. Add value, show kindness, give generously, have patience, and practice gratitude."

- Dupé Aleru

"If you're not where you want to be in life, then you need to step out of your conveniences and step into your priorities."

—————————————————————————————

- Dupé Aleru

"A wise person will use their opposition
to create new opportunities."

- *Dupé Aleru*

"You will not build trust with people if what you speak doesn't represent how you live your life."

- Dupé Aleru

"Be careful of giving your time to those that take away your peace. Choose instead to give your time to those who bring you the most peace."

- *Dupé Aleru*

"In the moments you feel like giving up, remember your higher purpose. You are still here for a reason, and you will discover that reason only when you keep moving forward."

- Dupé Aleru

"You are tested the most when you're about to step into your next level of success. This is where things may seem difficult, but do not give up because there's a challenge; instead, smile because you trust what's to come."

- Dupé Aleru

"The only thing standing between you and greatness is a limiting belief."

- Dupé Aleru

"Sometimes you will have to motivate others to motivate yourself."

– Dupé Aleru

"Letting go of a toxic relationship is courageous. Even if you stumble on your way out the door, you're out the door."

- Dupé Aleru

"Get clear on your goals, and that will build your confidence, which in turn will create the vision that will lead to action."

- Dupé Aleru

"Life will throw you a curveball. The goal is to be ready to catch it and throw it back."

- Dupé Aleru

"If you make consistency a lifestyle, then you will never stop until you reach your end goal."

- Dupé Aleru

"You were born to be great. Now is
the time to act like it."

- *Dupé Aleru*

"They once laughed at your dreams. Now they're begging to be in them."

- *Dupé Aleru*

"Try not to hold onto people that are not meant to join you on your journey. They may be the reason you don't make it to your destination."

- Dupé Aleru

"Set goals, create an action plan for achievement, be resourceful and flexible with the process, and don't stop until you achieve the outcome."

- Dupé Aleru

"Hitting rock bottom is a blessing in disguise because if you don't know what it is like at the bottom, then you cannot appreciate what lies at the top."

———————————————————————

- Dupé Aleru

"When you take a test, you must keep your eyes on your paper. When you go after your dreams, you mustn't compare yourself to other people."

- Dupé Aleru

"Some people are in long-distance relationships, living in the same house."

- Dupé Aleru

"The world has enough copycats.
The world needs more innovators."

- Dupé Aleru

"Every adversity you face will direct
you to where you need to be."

_____

- Dupé Aleru

"Shine your light so bright that you make some people squint and others buy shades."

- Dupé Aleru

"Knowing your purpose is believing in something bigger than yourself that no one can see but you and God."

– Dupé Aleru

"When you show people your worth, they will either rise to the occasion or leave."

- Dupé Aleru

"The most successful people see adversity not as a setback, but as a setup to their comeback."

— *Dupé Aleru*

"It is essential to hang around people who feed you, not leave you starving. Turn your life from an all-you-can-eat buffet to a potluck—people have to bring a dish to stay."

- Dupé Aleru

"Stop allowing the pressure of society, trends, or expectations keep you from doing what you were called to do. Be led by peace, not pressure."

- Dupé Aleru

"It is important that in those moments when your mind tells you to give up, your heart remembers why you started in the first place."

- Dupé Aleru

"Your wealth must start in your mind, or your bank account will remain the same."

- *Dupé Aleru*

"Clarity is the mother of success. You cannot get what you want until you know what you want and what you have to do to get it."

- *Dupé Aleru*

"When you intentionally go out of your way to not support others, you are planting seeds in bad soil, and what will harvest are weeds."

- Dupé Aleru

"Some people are quick to judge and slow to listen. Every statement does not require a reaction."

- Dupé Aleru

"Sometimes, the people who support you the most are the ones who know you the least."

- Dupé Aleru

"The moment you question if you can trust someone is the moment you have your answer."

- Dupé Aleru

"Sometimes you have to be sick and tired of being sick and tired before you begin to create change in your life."

- Dupé Aleru

"There is someone out there waiting for your gift, and they are unable to fulfill their purpose until you step into yours."

- Dupé Aleru

"The way you respond to your adversities determines the kind of person you will become."

- Dupé Aleru

"It's going to be difficult, but the challenge will strengthen you."

- Dupé Aleru

"You must learn how to stay focused because there will be people around you who know your worth, and they will try to distract you from your goals."

- Dupé Aleru

"Some people come into your life only to point you towards your purpose."

- Dupé Aleru

"Rejection doesn't mean you're
a bad person; it just means they
weren't YOUR person."

- *Dupé Aleru*

"Some people don't support you because they are unable to believe in possibilities for themselves, so they project their limiting beliefs onto you."

- Dupé Aleru

"You don't need answers—you have the answer. What you're seeking is a sign to validate your reasoning to stay because you are too scared to let go. But all that means is that you do not believe you deserve better."

- Dupé Aleru

"Stop falling into traps that set you backward,
but rather keep an eye out for opportunities
that will propel you forward."

- Dupé Aleru

"It doesn't make sense to bring sand to a beach, so do not bring someone who was meant to stay in your past into your future."

- *Dupé Aleru*

"It's okay to have love for the person who caused you the most pain, but loving them doesn't mean being with them. Sometimes you will have to say goodbye to people and love them from a distance."

- *Dupé Aleru*

Final Thoughts

You just finished reading this book, and I hope you're inspired to leap into the world and continue your transformational journey. But what if you're wondering, what do I do now?

I suggest that you spend time reflecting on where you were before reading this book, and where you are now that you've finished, and where you would like to be. Write your thoughts down.

Since you began reading *Daily Dose with Dupé: 100 quotes to help you jumpstart your day with positivity and inspiration*, have you been taking daily actionable steps towards your goals? If so, what have been some positive changes you've seen in your life? How have your morning rituals improved your overall well-being, relationships with others, and personal growth? What are some ways that you have held yourself accountable to your routines and goals? And if you have fallen off track, what can you do moving forward to ensure your commitment towards the things you want most out of life?

The best way to move forward is to appreciate your journey, the good and the bad. I constantly reflect on how far I've come to appreciate where I am now. Four years ago, I started Daily Dose with Dupé, a motivational video series that empowers, inspires, and educates people on topics about personal development, overcoming adversity, healing through relationships, making life-changing career and business moves, and more. The videos have allowed me to not only grow my brand, but more importantly, they have allowed me to connect with people all over the world that I wouldn't have had the pleasure of meeting otherwise. Thank you all for being a part of my journey and allowing me to live out my purpose by doing what I love the most—providing value through motivational speaking, coaching, and content creation.

I encourage you to keep moving forward no matter what obstacles appear on your path because the world awaits you, and you have a gift that someone needs. Be great and stay obedient to what you were called to do.

Acknowledgment

Enormous thanks to all the remarkable supporters I have had the opportunity to inspire, empower, and educate throughout the years; I want to say thank you for being the inspiration and heart for this collection of my favorite sayings meant to help bring positivity and inspiration into your lives. I especially want to thank my parents, Joseph and Joyin Aleru, for always encouraging me to go after my dreams. I love you both so much, and I thank God every day for blessing me with two loving and supportive parents. Finally, to those who have been a part of this book's creation process: Faith Clancy and Allison Doyle.

Other Works by Dupé

Animals in Action A-Z

SCALE High
Teacher's Manual

SCALE High Student
Workbook

SCALE High Goal
Setting Guide and
Weekly Journal

Speak Up!

User's Guide

Made in the USA
Coppell, TX
26 January 2022

72403921R00063